THROUGH THE BIBLE IN SIX CHAPTERS

Kit Sublett

Whitecaps Media
Houston, Texas
whitecapsmedia.com

Through the Bible in Six Chapters
© 2015 Kit Sublett
All rights reserved

ISBN: 978-1-942732-00-6

Unless otherwise noted, Scripture quotations are from the ESV® Bible (*The Holy Bible, English Standard Version®*), copyright © 2001 by Crossway Bibles, a publishing ministry of Good News Publishers. Used by permission. All rights reserved

Scripture quotations marked NLT are taken from the *Holy Bible*, New Living Translation, copyright © 1996, 2004, 2007, 2013 by Tyndale House Foundation. Used by permission of Tyndale House Publishers, Inc., Carol Stream, Illinois 60188. All rights reserved

Scripture quotations marked "NIV 1984" are taken from the Holy Bible, New International Version®. NIV®. Copyright © 1973, 1978, 1984 by Biblica, Inc. Used by permission of Zondervan. All rights reserved worldwide

Quotation designated (NET) is from the NET Bible® copyright © 1996-2006 by Biblical Studies Press, L.L.C. http://netbible.com All rights reserved

For information on bulk purchases of this book, please visit whitecapsmedia.com

Printed in the United States of America

Table of Contents

STUDY 1 Genesis 1 5

STUDY 2 Genesis 3 20

STUDY 3 Exodus 12 34

STUDY 4 John 3 46

STUDY 5 Mark 15 59

STUDY 6 Romans 12 75

Download the Study Guide for this book at **whitecapsmedia.com**

Study 1

Genesis 1

The Bible is a wonderful book. No, let me rephrase that: The Bible isn't just a wonderful book, it is *the* Book. It has sold more copies than any book ever written and continues to do so, year after year, decade after decade, and century after century. It has been praised, read, discussed, memorized, and challenged more than any other book. Many people over the centuries have even gone to their deaths to ensure that we have copies available to us in our language.

It is also a really big book. Just look at your own copy. How many pages does it have? You may never have read a book that long before.

As you probably already know—and if you don't, it's easy enough to observe by just thumbing through your copy—the Bible comes in two sections: a longer section we know as the Old Testament, followed by a shorter section we call the New Testament.

The Bible, both testaments, center around one figure: Jesus Christ. The Old Testament looks forward to His coming and was written before Jesus' birth in Bethlehem, and the New Testament tells His story and was written after He had returned to heaven. Jesus is both the dividing line between the two testaments and also the bridge connecting the two.

Of course there is much more to the Bible than just Jesus, but don't ever lose sight of the fact that He is its focus. Sometimes, particularly in the Old Testament, He's a little harder to see—the name "Jesus" doesn't even appear—but He's there. Here's how Jesus Himself put it: "You search the Scriptures because you think that in them you have eternal life; and it is they that bear witness about me" (John 5:38).

Every intelligent person, and certainly every Christian, needs to read the Bible—the whole thing—in their lifetime. It has impacted more of humanity and culture than any other single influence. My rule of thumb is that every Christian should have read through the New Testament within the first two years of being a believer, and through the entire Bible within the first five years of being a believer. And then they should keep on reading it! You will never regret spending time in God's Word. As Moses said in Deuteronomy, "It is no empty word for you, but your very life" (Deuteronomy 32:47).

Through the Bible in Six Chapters is no substitute for reading the whole Bible, of course, but sometimes it's easier to digest a new movie or book by having an overview of where the story is going. As I said, the Bible is a big book, and it can be daunting. The purpose of this six-session study is to take a quick tour through the Bible by looking at a single chapter each time. By doing so, my hope is that you get a brief overview of the whole Bible and will be encouraged to read the entire thing for yourself.

So let's get started. And where would be the best place to begin a study of the Bible? How about the very first chapter of the very first book?

Appropriately, that book is called Genesis, and if you look up *genesis* in a dictionary you will find that it means "the beginning" or "the origin." Genesis gets its name not only because it's the first book of the Bible but also because it is a book all about origins. The beginning of the universe, of life itself, of the human race, of sin, of God's relationship with man, of the people of God, and even of Christ's involvement with the human story—it's all in there! Because of that, it's an incredibly important book in understanding the Christian faith.

So, let's begin with Genesis, chapter one, verse one. There have been a lot of famous "first lines" in literature. Here are some of my favorites:

"Call me Ishmael" (the first line of *Moby Dick*).

"It was the best of times, it was the worst of times..." (*A Tale of Two Cities*)

"If you really want to know about it, the first thing you'll probably want to know is where I was born, and what my lousy childhood was like ... " (*The Catcher in the Rye*)

But the most famous opening line of all is Genesis 1:1: "In the beginning, God created the heavens and the earth." I imagine that more people have read that first line than any other first line of any other book in history.

"In the beginning"—what a great way to start for a book that is about the origin of everything!

I want to pick this line apart. We won't do this with every chapter we look at in these six studies, seeing that there about 800,000 words in the Bible and to study them word by word would take more than the amount of time we have! But take a look at those first four words:

"In the beginning, God ..."

What do those seemingly simple four words tell us about God?

Here are two important things that come to my mind: First, they tell us that God was *before* everything. Second, they indicate that He is the *cause* of everything.

God is "pre-existent." You might not have heard that term before. It means that He comes before everything and that He is not bound by time. Take a look at what Psalm 90:2 tells us about God: "Before the mountains were brought forth, or ever you had formed the earth and the world, from everlasting to everlasting, you are God."

If God is not bound by time (and Scripture tells us that He is not), that means He is different from us and that time has no effect on Him. He is, in fact, eternal, existing before time began and after time will end.

Do you know an elderly person, perhaps a grandparent? If you are around them on a regular basis, you can see the effect of time on them greatly. Day by day they get weaker; maybe they lose their hearing or their vision. It's a sad thing to see and it's a hard thing to go through for the aging person. "Old age ain't for sissies," I once heard someone observe. Time takes its toll on everyone. But while that will be true for all of us, it will not be true of God! Why not? Because He is not bound by time. He never runs out of it. He is time's Master. He can see the future as well as the present and the past. He is not limited to one place or time.

Getting back to our first verse, let's add the next word: "In the beginning, God created …"

Sometimes when we hear something over and over we no longer consider what it means. I imagine we've all heard "In the beginning, God created" many times. But I want to encourage you to slow down and think about the implications of the idea that God created "in the beginning."

During my years on the staff of Young Life, the ministry bought a large chunk of land outside Winter Park, Colorado. It eventually became Young Life's Crooked Creek Ranch, an incredible showplace for the proclamation of the gospel to high school students. But when we bought it, it was nothing but raw land. There were no roads, no electricity, no telephone wires, no sewage or water systems, and no buildings. It was just lots of beautiful land. I was privileged to visit the site many times "in the beginning."

But in Genesis, when it says "in the beginning," it means that there was *nothing* there to start with. At least Crooked Creek had land. In the Creation, God had nothing to work with. When God created, He was making something out of nothing. Perhaps you've heard the expression, "to create something out of thin air." Well, God didn't even have air—thin or otherwise—with which to work.

Further, "In the beginning, God created" means that God is the origin of everything, that He is the Creator, Giver, and Sustainer of Life.

We are reminded of this in the very last book of the Bible, Revelation. "Worthy are you, our Lord and God, to receive glory and honor and power, for you created all things, and by your will they existed and were created" (Revelation 4:11). Further, we learn in Colossians 1:16–17 that "by [Christ] all things were created, in heaven and on earth ... And he is before all things, and in him all things hold together."

It has been pointed out that those first five words— "In the beginning, God created"—also tell us that life can have meaning and purpose. If that doesn't immediately seem like a logical conclusion to you, consider the alternative.

What is the alternative to there being a Creator God? Simply, that there is *not* a Creator God, and therefore what we experience is not a creation but instead is some sort of fluke or accident. Right? You can't have design if you do not have a Designer.

Rebecca Pippert, in her book *Out of the Saltshaker*, told the following story:

> I had a biology professor who stated the first day of class, "Man is merely a fortuitous concourse of

atoms, a meaningless piece of protoplasm in an absurd world." We were taught that having deep regard for random products of the universe where chance is king was inconsistent. Some time later he told our class in despair that his 13-year-old daughter had run away to live with an older man. "She will be deeply wounded. She will scar, and I can't do anything to help. I must sit back and watch a tragedy," he said grimly.

I raised my hand and said, quietly, that according to his system protoplasm would not scar.

His answer was devastating. "Touché. I could never regard my daughter as a set of chemicals, never. I can't take my beliefs that far. Class dismissed."

The good news from Genesis 1, however is that there *is* a Creator. And if there is a Creator, then we can and almost certainly do have a purpose.

I remember being frustrated in high school when my English teachers would talk about foreshadowing and hidden meaning in books. For some reason that seemed ludicrous to me (maybe that said more about my own attitude toward reading assignments than anything else!). I felt the same way in college when I took an art history course and the professor went on and on about the meanings of famous paintings and the detail in their layout and artistry. "Sure, whatever," I thought.

Years later I happened to be in the most famous art museum in the world, the Louvre in Paris. I was admiring a large painting and I noticed a small dog painted in the corner of the picture. The dog had no apparent significance, it was simply part of the overall scene. All of the sudden a basic thought hit me: There is nothing in this painting that the artist did not put there, including the dog. We may not understand the purpose—in fact, the purpose may have been trivial—but the artist felt like the painting would not be complete unless he added the dog to the picture.

Nothing could exist in that painting—or any painting—unless the artist took the time and thought to put it there. The same can be said of any creative endeavor: When a chef cooks a dish, he does it just so and has a reason for every ingredient. The same goes for television shows, computers, and houses. And, much to my chagrin, as I began to write books as an adult, I realized that my English teachers had been correct all along: Nothing gets on a piece of paper that the author does not put there, that authors really do take time to put in foreshadowing and symbolism. Any created thing exists because its creator put it there.

Just as the artist put the dog in the painting for a reason, so we were created for a reason. And because there is a Creator God, we can have meaning and purpose. If there is no God and if we were not created, then ultimately we have no meaning and cannot have purpose.

Continuing with this first verse, let's finish the whole sentence: "In the beginning, God created the heavens and the earth." What does that tell us about God's relationship with the universe? If God created the universe—"the heavens and the earth"—it means He is before and above it all. It is not just humanity that God created—it's everything! And God stands supreme over all of it.

By now we've managed to cover one whole verse. Let's pick up the pace a little bit and look at the next several verses:

> The earth was without form and void, and darkness was over the face of the deep. And the Spirit of God was hovering over the face of the waters.
>
> And God said, "Let there be light," and there was light. And God saw that the light was good. And God separated the light from the darkness. God called the

light Day, and the darkness he called Night. And there was evening and there was morning, the first day.

(Genesis 1:2–5)

It is interesting to me that the Bible mentions light so early on. We know how vital light is to life. Plants and humans cannot survive without it. Indeed, as I was writing this book I read an article that scientists at Harvard had used laser light to trigger the growth of teeth. Light is absolutely critical to life as we know it! Long before science had figured any of this out, the Bible was talking about it.

Looking back on verses 2–5, do you notice what the entire earth consisted of? Just water. I find that interesting as well, because it seems like scientists are always saying that life began in water. In that case, the Bible and the scientists are in agreement. So where did the land come from? The next verses explain that.

> And God said, "Let there be an expanse in the midst of the waters, and let it separate the waters from the waters." And God made the expanse and separated the waters that were under the expanse from the waters that were above the expanse. And it was so.

And God called the expanse Heaven. And there was evening and there was morning, the second day.

And God said, "Let the waters under the heavens be gathered together into one place, and let the dry land appear." And it was so. God called the dry land Earth, and the waters that were gathered together he called Seas. And God saw that it was good.

(Genesis 1:6–10)

Looking back over those first several verses (and specifically verses 3 through 10), do you see how God creates? What mechanism He uses? Notice the pattern over the first two days of creation:

- v. 3: "And God said, 'Let there be light' …"
- v. 6: "And God said, 'Let there be an expanse …'"
- v. 9: "And God said, 'Let the waters under the heavens be gathered together …"

The mechanism He uses is His voice: He speaks, and it happens! God continues this pattern throughout Genesis 1:

- on Day 3 He creates vegetation
- on Day 4 He creates stars and "lights of day and night" (the sun and moon)
- on Day 5 He creates fish and birds

- on Day 6 He creates land animals (He created something else on Day 6, Man, and we'll talk about that in a second)

The pattern is, "And God said … and it was so." Then, at the end of the creative process, God observes something. He sees that it is "good." In fact, at the end of the chapter, the last verse reads, "And God saw everything that he had made, and behold it was very good."

The fact that God "saw that it was good" makes a significant statement about the created world: not only that God created it, but also that He takes pleasure in His creation and that it was good, or without blemish. The world was perfect, and God enjoyed it.

Now, as promised, let's take a look at the creation of mankind. We find that talked about in verses 26–27:

> Then God said, "Let us make man in our image, after our likeness. And let them have dominion over the fish of the sea and over the birds of the heavens and over the livestock and over all the earth and over every creeping thing that creeps on the earth."
>
> So God created man in his own image, in the image of God he created him, male and female he created them. *(Genesis 1:26–27)*

There is a whole lot in just those two short verses but as we wrap up this study I just want to point out a few.

The first is that verse 26 makes an important distinction between mankind and God's other creations from that day. Do you see what it is? It is that we are created in His image. Not only that, but the wording is very specific: it goes out of its way to point out that both man *and* woman are in His image.

Have you ever thought of how we are like God? I can think of several ways. We have spoken language. We have relationships. We are capable of reason. We are capable of morality. Finally, we are creative. Not all of the creatures God created have those attributes—many have none—and we are the only ones that have them all. We are truly created in God's likeness.

The fact that mankind is created in God's image has important implications. It means that all people have worth—no one, not a single person, is an accident. It means that we have a purpose. And the fact that we alone in all of creation are made in God's image means that mankind is uniquely special to God.

There is one other thing I want to point out in this chapter. Look back at verse 26: "Then God said, 'Let us make man in *our* image, after *our* likeness'" (emphasis mine). Who is He talking about there? Who is involved in the plural word "our"? There are a few theories, but I like to think this is the first reference to the Trinity, that we are made in the image of God the Father, Son, and Holy Spirit.

Which leads me to the last point I want to make about this first chapter of Scripture. Trinitarian allusions aside, Genesis 1 establishes firmly the idea of monotheism. That may not seem like a big deal to us, as Western Civilization has firmly been in the camp of monotheism for centuries, but it is a vitally important principle. God is One. The Bible does not teach multiple gods like many religions currently do (and all other religions did at the time the Bible was written). We do not have a god of the harvest and a god of war and a god of love. We have one God—the Creator God of Genesis 1, who made all there is and lastly created us, in His image, for His pleasure.

Study 2

Genesis 3

If we're going to make it through the entire Bible in six chapters, we need to get moving. So we're going to move from Genesis 1 all the way to Genesis 3. We're picking up the pace!

Before we get going on Genesis 3 I want to make a strong suggestion to you. It's a simple one, but if you do it, it will change your life. Here it is: Read your Bible daily, and for the rest of your life. That's it. Decades of experience walking with the Lord has taught me that spending time in God's Word regularly will do more to help you and strengthen you than just about anything else you can do.

Jesus knew that, and told us so in Matthew 4:4. Quoting the Old Testament, He said, "It is written, 'Man shall not live by bread alone, but by every word that comes from the mouth of God.'"

Jesus is very deliberate in His wording here. You wouldn't dream of missing a meal, much less go a whole day without food, and He is telling us that just as important as physical food is to our well-being, so is spiritual food. There's only one place to get that food: studying God's Word. When you're finished with this book, I hope that you will continue to study the Bible on your own. You'll be glad you did!

I would go so far as to say that if you are not reading God's Word on a regular basis you are not a serious Christian. Did that sting? Maybe it needs to. Don't just get your Bible off the shelf (or out of your glove compartment) for your weekly Bible study or Sunday mornings. The great nineteenth-century English preacher and author J. C. Ryle was fond of reciting the question Jesus asked in Luke 10:26—"What is written in the Law? How do you read it?"—and then expanding on it by asking: *"What are you doing with the Bible? How do you read it?"*

There are many obstacles people have when it comes to getting in the habit of daily Bible study, but all of them have easy solutions.

Find it too difficult to understand? Get one of the many easy-to-understand translations available at any bookstore or online.

Find reading long passages difficult? Okay, then read a smaller amount. A typical chapter of the Bible is not very long. If that's too long, then read half of it one day and the rest the next.

Not sure where to start? I always tell people to start with the Gospel of Mark in the New Testament. There are any number of reading plans available. An older Christian can help you here.

Find it dull? Then until you get the hang of it, stick to the Gospel accounts and the other narrative portions of the Bible.

Enough of my soapbox. Just remember how the Bible describes itself: "All Scripture is breathed out by God and profitable for teaching, for reproof, for correction, and for training in righteousness, that the man of God may be competent, equipped for every good work" (2 Timothy 3:16–17). You need it to live your life the way God wants you to!

Now let's move into our next chapter, Genesis 3.

In Genesis 1, we saw that God created the world, the universe, and mankind, and He declared it all "good." But like any good story, there needs to be some conflict, and Genesis 3 introduces the greatest conflict in human history. In fact, the events described in it are so pivotal the chapter actually has a name—it is often called "The Fall of Man"—and it is the saddest chapter in all of Scripture. It shapes everything that is to come. Had the events of chapter 3 not occurred, the Bible would have been complete at only two chapters, Genesis 1 and 2. Everything that follows—from Genesis 4 through Revelation 22—is as a result of the events we're about to study.

Before we get into chapter 3, there are a few verses in the previous chapter we need to consider:

> The LORD God took the man and put him in the garden of Eden to work it and keep it. And the LORD God commanded the man, saying, "You may surely eat of every tree of the garden, but of the tree of the knowledge of good and evil you shall not eat, for in the day that you eat of it you shall surely die."
>
> *(Genesis 2:15–17)*

Keep that in mind as we begin with the first several verses of chapter 3:

> Now the serpent was more crafty than any other beast of the field that the LORD God had made.
>
> He said to the woman, "Did God actually say, 'You shall not eat of any tree in the garden?'" And the woman said to the serpent, "We may eat of the fruit of the trees in the garden, but God said, 'You shall

not eat of the fruit of the tree that is in the midst of the garden, neither shall you touch it, lest you die.'" But the serpent said to the woman, "You will not surely die. For God knows that when you eat of it your eyes will be opened, and you will be like God, knowing good and evil." *(Genesis 3:1–5)*

Look back at verse 1. Do you see what the serpent is doing to the woman? He is causing her to doubt what God had said; in effect, to doubt God's Word. "Did God *actually* say … ?" If a friend of yours begins a question with "Did she *really* say …?" you know that your friend is questioning what you heard.

Now, notice when the woman answers the serpent, she sort of gets God's instructions correct (see vv. 2:15–17), but she adds to it.

The serpent continues to cast doubt about what God has said. You can almost hear him laughing as he challenges the woman. "Ha! You will not surely die!"

Of course, we now know that the serpent was none other than Satan. Genesis 3 marks his first appearance in Scripture, but he will make many more. One of his names is the great deceiver (see Revelation 12:9) and it is appropriate that his first appearance shows him attempting (and succeeding) to deceive Eve. Specifically, his two deceptions in these verses are that you will not die, and that Adam and Eve would be like God.

And then, the Fall:

> So when the woman saw that the tree was good for food, and that it was a delight to the eyes, and that the tree was to be desired to make one wise, she took of its fruit and ate, and she also gave some to her husband who was with her, and he ate. Then the eyes of both were opened, and they knew that they were naked. And they sewed fig leaves together and made themselves loincloths. *(Genesis 3:6–7)*

Upon looking at the tree God had warned Adam about, Eve found three desirable things. First, it was good for food; second, it was delightful to the eyes; and third, it was able to provide wisdom. (In some ways, the tree bore the same temptations that make sex outside of marriage attractive: it looked good and delightful, and promised to make the participant somehow more mature and worldly-wise.)

Looking at verse 7 we see the first result of Adam and Eve's disobedience to God: "Then the eyes of both were opened, and they knew that they were naked." As a result, they felt shame and tried to hide it by covering their loins with fig leaves. And while shame was an immediate consequence of their disobedience, notice what was not: unlike Satan's promise to Eve, they did not become equal to God.

Verses 8–13 continue the story:

> And they heard the sound of the LORD God walking in the garden in the cool of the day, and the man and his wife hid themselves from the presence of the LORD God among the trees of the garden. But the LORD God called to the man and said to him, "Where are you?" And he said, "I heard the sound of you in the garden, and I was afraid, because I was naked, and I hid myself." He said, "Who told you that you were naked? Have you eaten of the tree of which I commanded you not to eat?" The man said, "The woman whom you gave to be with me, she gave me fruit of the tree, and I ate." Then the LORD God said to the woman, "What is this that you have done? The woman said, "The serpent deceived me, and I ate."
>
> *(Genesis 3:8–13)*

In verses 8 and 9 they are trying to hide from God. This would be sort of funny if it did not depict something so sad. Up to this point, life on earth had been idyllic. There was harmony between Adam and Eve, and most importantly between the two of them and their Maker. Life was literally perfect. But when they go against God's one instruction to them, they immediately and instinctively know that something has changed. As a result, they hide.

While it might be easy to look objectively at Adam and Eve and see the futility of trying to hide from God, I think we often do the same thing ourselves. We do something we know to be contrary to God's best for us, some kind of sin, and before you know it we are hiding from God. We're not literally running into the closet or into the forest. Our 21st century hiding is much more sophisticated than that. We feel ashamed and so we take ourselves out of fellowship with other believers. We stop going to church or to our Bible study group. And most of all we avoid direct contact with God. At the time when we need Him most, we are running away from Him.

In the garden, God confronts Adam. "Where are you?" This reminds me of a scene that is played out daily between parents and young children and no doubt happened to all of us when we were little. A loving parent knows instinctively when something is wrong. And, as is so often the case between a parent and a young child, the parent already knows what is really the matter, but he or she just wants to hear what the child has to say about it. Like a small child, Adam just makes it worse. He tells his Father that he is afraid of Him and that he felt the need to hide.

"Who told you that you were naked?" God asks, knowing full well how this occurred. "Have you eaten of the tree of which I commanded you not to eat?"

This scene quickly degrades into a blame game of historic proportion. The woman blames the serpent, refusing to take responsibility for her part in the disobedience. After all, the serpent deceived her. "I'm just a victim," she seems to be saying. But the only reason she is offering this pitiful excuse is because the man has already thrown her under the bus, blaming her and in doing so manages to ever so subtly blame God Himself! "Well, the woman gave me the fruit—you know, the woman that *You* gave me."

Just as we often imitate Adam and Eve in trying to hide from God, I think we also imitate our original ancestors in not taking responsibility for our sin. Think of the excuses we throw out: "Everyone else was doing it!" "I felt peer pressure!" "I'm just geared that way!" "I was tired!" God has heard them all, and I can just imagine Him shaking His head in sadness each and every time we trot out these tired, worn-out excuses. Who is responsible for our own sin? Only ourselves. We cannot play the blame game or claim to be a victim. We need to own up to our responsibility.

God had heard enough, and now it was time to tell the three parties involved—Adam, Eve, and the serpent—the consequences of their actions. They are consequences that reverberate to this day.

First up was the serpent:

> The LORD God said to the serpent, "Because you have done this, cursed are you above all the livestock and above all beasts of the field; on your belly you shall go, and dust you shall eat all the days of your life.
>
> "I will put enmity between you and the woman, and between your offspring and her offspring; he shall bruise your head, and you shall bruise his heel."
>
> *(Genesis 3:14–15)*

So the punishment that God metes out to the serpent is that he will crawl on the ground and eat dust. But there is an even more important prophecy that God makes. Verse 15 has a fancy name: it is called the *protoevangelium*. (If you want to impress your friends you can throw that around at their next party. But before you do you will want to know just what it means.) *Proto* means "first in time, earliest" and *evangelium* means "good news," so *protoevangelium* means "the first good news" or "the first gospel." Many theologians believe that this single verse is God's first promise to us of our eventual Savior, Jesus. Satan will wage war against man, but eventually Eve's descendant, Jesus, will crush his head. (Some people just say it explains why we people have a problem with snakes, but I think God had something bigger in mind.)

Next up for her punishment was the woman:

> To the woman he said, "I will surely multiply your pain in childbearing; in pain you shall bring forth children. Your desire shall be for your husband, and he shall rule over you." *(Genesis 3:16)*

Another translation, the NET Bible, translates that last phrase this way: "You will want to control your husband, but he will dominate you."

However it is translated, the consequences to the woman and her descendants are clear: pain in childbearing, and tension between husbands and wives.

Adam does not get off easy, either:

And to Adam he said, "Because you have listened to the voice of your wife and have eaten of the tree of which I commanded you, 'You shall not eat of it,' cursed is the ground because of you; in pain you shall eat of it all the days of your life; thorns and thistles it shall bring forth for you; and you shall eat the plants of the field. By the sweat of your face you shall eat bread, till you return to the ground, for out of it you were taken; for you are dust, and to dust you shall return." *(Genesis 3:17–19)*

Work in and of itself is a good thing. God works, and did so even before the events of chapter 3, He set man to work (in chapter 2, God "took the man and put him in the garden of Eden to work it and keep it"). So work was not a consequence of the Fall, but difficulty in work was. No longer would Adam and Eve be able to just enjoy the abundance of the garden; instead, the man would have to toil for it. The next time you have difficulty doing something, blame Adam!

The biggest consequence of all was what is implied in verse 19: death. "For you are dust" (which refers back to Genesis 2:7), "and to dust you shall return," that is, die. Romans 5:12 clarifies the meaning of this when it explains that "when Adam sinned, sin entered the world. Adam's sin brought death, so death spread to everyone, for everyone sinned" (NLT).

I said at the outset that this is the saddest chapter of the entire Bible. I hope you see now why I would describe it that way. If you ever wanted to know whatever happened to the Garden of Eden, the final verses give us the rest of the story.

> The man called his wife's name Eve, because she was the mother of all living. And the LORD God made for Adam and for his wife garments of skin and clothed them.
>
> Then the LORD God said, "Behold, the man has become like us in knowing good and evil. Now, lest he reach out his hand and take also of the tree of life and eat, and live forever—" therefore the LORD God sent him out from the garden of Eden to work the ground from which he was taken. He drove out the man, and at the east of the garden of Eden he placed the cherubim and a flaming sword that turned every way to guard the way to the tree of life.
>
> *(Genesis 3:20–24)*

A few notes to end on. In Hebrew, *Adam* means "man," and *Eve* means "life-giver," very appropriate names for the first human and for his wife, the first person who would bring another life into the world. Second, in verse 21 God makes provision for man's sin. He does it by killing an animal. This is a foreshadowing not only of Christ's eventual sacrifice, but also of the sacrificial system in place in much of the Old Testament.

From the excellent *Bible Knowledge Commentary*, note the differences between man's existence before the Fall and after it. Before the Fall, he had life; after, he had death. Before, he had pleasure; after, he had pain. Before, he had abundance; after, he had meager subsistence. Before, he had perfect fellowship with both his wife and with God; after, he had alienation and conflict.

For the rest of time, until Christ comes back, the legacy of Adam and Eve will be felt by all of us who are their offspring.

Study 3

Exodus 12

Our story has progressed quite a bit in only two chapters. God has created the entire world and humankind and declared them good. But then man threw everything out of kilter by disobeying God and bringing sin into the world.

As I commented in the last study, the entire rest of the Bible exists because of the events of Genesis 3. The rest of the story of the Bible will be the story of man's sin and his broken relationship with God.

God, being God, had a plan all along, as hinted at in one of the final verses of Genesis 3. You can see it in verse 21: "And the LORD God made for Adam and his wife garments of skin and clothed them."

God sacrificed some animals in order to cover over the shame of the humans. The forgiveness of sins is a constant theme in both the Old and New testaments and it always involves the shedding of blood, of sacrifice, of death (in the case of Genesis 3:21, the death of the animals whose skin was used).

This sacrificial system—which as we will see was in itself a mere foreshadowing of the ultimate sacrifice—developed over the centuries following Adam and Eve. By the time we get to today's chapter, Exodus 12, God had instituted a very sophisticated system of sacrificial offerings to forgive His people's sins. But it's important to understand that the sacrificial system of the Old Testament was merely looking forward to and a picture of the sacrifice made by Christ.

Before we get into today's chapter we need to set some context, as much has happened over the centuries between Adam and Eve and Exodus 12. The main thing to know is that by this time God has chosen a race of people, the Israelites (or Jews), to be His own people. They are the ones through whom God was going to bless the world with a Savior.

The Jews were led by a man named Moses, one of the most significant figures not only in the Bible but also in human history. His statue is in the Library of Congress, movies have been made about his life, countless books written about him, and he is revered by Jews and Christians alike. He was a great hero and a fascinating figure. It is believed that he wrote the first five books of the Bible. Most importantly, he is the one to whom God gave the Ten Commandments (hence his nickname, "The Lawgiver").

By the time Exodus 12 begins, the Jewish people are enslaved in Egypt and God has appointed Moses to lead them out of bondage (see Exodus 3:7–10). The book of Exodus (the name means "exit") tells the story of their deliverance from slavery and their exit out of Egypt.

If you look at a Bible that has section headings, you'll see some intriguing entries beginning around Exodus 7:14. My old NIV Study Bible has these: the plague of blood, the plague of frogs, the plague of gnats, the plague of flies, the plague on livestock, the plague of boils, the plague of hail, the plague of locusts, the plague of darkness, and finally, the plague on the firstborn. As a kid I always found these chapters really interesting!

You might wonder what was the point of all of those afflictions on Egypt. Of course the best place to find out would be to read those chapters yourself, but I'll give you the quick version here: Before each plague, Moses went to the Pharaoh and implored him to release the Jews from their slavery and let them go back to their Promised Land (what we now know as Israel). Each time, the Pharaoh stubbornly refused, and each time his refusal was met by one of the plagues.

The worst plague is the last one, the plague on the firstborn. Here's how it is described in Exodus 11:4–9:

So Moses said, "Thus says the LORD: 'About midnight I will go out in the midst of Egypt, and every firstborn in the land of Egypt shall die, from the firstborn of Pharaoh who sits on his throne, even to the firstborn of the slave girl who is behind the handmill, and all the firstborn of the cattle. There shall be a great cry throughout all the land of Egypt, such as there has never been, nor ever will be again. But not a dog shall growl against any of the people of Israel, either man or beast, that you may know that the LORD makes a distinction between Egypt and Israel.' And all these your servants shall come down to me and bow down to me, saying, 'Get out, you and all the people who follow you.' And after that I will go out." And he went out from Pharaoh in hot anger. Then the LORD said to Moses, "Pharaoh will not listen to you, that my wonders may be multiplied in the land of Egypt."

Now we're ready for chapter 12. Let's see the provision that God is going to make for His people.

The first six verses are God giving Moses some instructions. They include that—

- each household needs to sacrifice a lamb
- the lambs to be sacrificed should be without blemish

- and the lambs are to be ceremonially slaughtered.

Earlier I mentioned the sacrificial system that God had put in place. It is summed up in Leviticus 17:11: "For the life of the body is in its blood. I have given you the blood on the altar to purify you, making you right with the LORD. It is the blood, given in exchange for a life, that makes purification possible" (NLT).

Hebrews 9:22 sums it up as well: "Indeed, under the law almost everything is purified with blood, and without the shedding of blood there is no forgiveness of sins."

Have you ever wondered why God is so serious about sin? Our culture, on the face of things, does not seem to take it very seriously. People laugh at God's standards, mocking even the notion of sin. But I think even the most jaded person takes sin seriously—at least when it is done *against* him or her. If we are robbed or a loved one is hurt by someone else, we care very much about sin. If a girlfriend or boyfriend cheats on us, we take their sin very seriously. If we see an injustice done or, worst of all, a murder take place, we expect that sin to be punished. Of course we must own up to the fact that we are guilty of sin ourselves. None of us are free of guilt.

I would also add that we *want* God to take sin seriously. Because if He does not—if He were to just look the other way and sweep it under the rug—then He ceases to be righteous and perfect. We don't want a God who is imperfect. That would make Him no better than we are. There could be no ultimate justice if God were imperfect, nor could there be a true spiritual standard.

God is holy and righteous and He cannot abide sin and will not allow it in His kingdom. So, as we have seen, from the very beginning of the human experience, He has provided a substitution for our punishment, specifically, the shedding of blood.

Now let's get back to chapter 12. Now that the Israelites have sacrificed their lambs, God gives them their next instructions:

> [God said,] "Then they shall take some of the blood and put it on the two doorposts and the lintel of the houses in which they eat it ... In this manner you shall eat it: with your belt fastened, your sandals on your feet, and your staff in your hand. And you shall eat it in haste. It is the LORD's Passover."
>
> *(Exodus 12:7, 11)*

You have almost certainly heard of Passover, as it is still celebrated by Jewish people all over the world as one of their holiest days. To this day they commemorate the events that are about to unfold in Exodus 12. (You might remember that Passover always falls around Easter; that is because, in the ultimate symbolism, Jesus went to the cross during Passover week. Therefore, Passover and Easter are always near each other on the calendar.)

The reason this celebration has the name "Passover" is explained in the next few verses:

> [God said] "For I will pass through the land of Egypt that night, and I will strike all the firstborn in the land of Egypt, both man and beast; and on all the gods of Egypt I will execute judgements: I am the LORD. The blood shall be a sign for you, on the houses where you are. And when I see the blood, I will pass over you, and no plague will befall you to destroy you, when I strike the land of Egypt."
>
> *(Exodus 12:12–13)*

It is called "Passover" because God was going to pass over the houses that were marked by the blood of the sacrificed lambs. Those houses that had the blood of a lamb over their doorposts would be passed over and saved.

Let's see what happened that night in Egypt:

> At midnight the LORD struck down all the firstborn in the land of Egypt, from the firstborn of Pharaoh who sat on his throne to the firstborn of the captive who was in the dungeon, and all the firstborn of the livestock. *(Exodus 12:29)*

It is almost impossible to imagine how horrible that night was. If only the Pharaoh had listened and obeyed God's order! He had been given chance after chance, but he did not, and God kept His word, as He always does. This is what happened next:

> And Pharaoh rose up in the night, he and all his servants and all the Egyptians. And there was a great cry in Egypt, for there was not a house where someone was not dead. Then he summoned Moses and Aaron by night and said, "Up, go out from among my people, both you and the people of Israel; and go, serve the LORD, as you have said. Take your flocks and your herds, as you have said, and be gone, and bless me also!" *(Exodus 12:30–32)*

Finally, after all of those plagues, Pharaoh relents and lets Moses lead his people out of Egypt. The actual exodus takes place next.

The Egyptians were urgent with the people to send them out of the land in haste. For they said, "We shall all be dead." So the people took their dough before it was leavened, their kneading bowls being bound up in their cloaks on their shoulders. The people of Israel had also done as Moses told them, for they had asked the Egyptians for silver and gold jewelry and for clothing. And the LORD had given the people favor in the sight of the Egyptians, so that they let them have what they asked. Thus they plundered the Egyptians.

And the people of Israel journeyed from Remeses to Succoth, about six hundred thousand men on foot, besides women and children.

(Exodus 12:33–37)

Israel is finally and magnificently free from bondage, and that is what the Jewish people celebrate on Passover (and also why they use unleavened bread— the Israelites' departure came so quickly they did not have time for the bread to rise). But Christians find even more significance in Passover, as we see it as a foreshadowing of the ultimate provision for sin: the death of Christ.

There are many parallels between the original Passover experience of Exodus 12 and the story of Christ's crucifixion (which itself took place during the celebration of Passover). You might enjoy seeing how many you can think of. These parallels are no accident, as God orchestrated both events.

I want to highlight a few. The first is the use of a lamb as a sacrifice (and not just any lamb, but one that was "without blemish"). Lambs were a common animal for Jews to use in their sacrifices, and certainly the one specifically called for in Exodus 12. Any Jew would know the link between Passover and lambs. Now look at how John the Baptist, a devout Jew, described Jesus: "The next day [John the Baptist] saw Jesus coming toward him, and said, 'Behold, the Lamb of God, who takes away the sin of the world!'" This was no idle turn of a phrase, but a God-given recognition of Jesus' special role. And notice that Jesus is not just any lamb, He is the Lamb of God and He will take away not just one family's sin (as was the case with each lamb in Exodus 12), but that of the whole world.

Like the lambs of Exodus 12, Jesus was sacrificed for the sins of others. But the similarity doesn't just end with Jesus' role. It also includes our response.

God warned Pharaoh that death was going to come to his nation. God still warns us about that. Romans 6:23 reminds us that "the wages of sin is death." Just like Pharaoh, we have been warned. But just like the people in Egypt, we too have been provided a way out.

In the Passover, the way people avoided death was to apply the blood of the sacrificed lamb to the doorposts of their homes. In the same way, we are to apply the blood of the Lamb to the doorposts of our lives—our hearts—through faith. Romans 6:23 in its entirety says, "For the wages of sin is death, but the free gift of God is eternal life in Christ Jesus our Lord."

We'll learn more about Jesus in our next chapter. Before we do that, though, I hope you've learned enough to place your faith in Him as the Lamb of God, who is the perfect atoning sacrifice for your sin.

Christ died to set us free from the bondage of sin and also from death. Here's how John, one of Jesus' closest friends, put it:

> And this is the testimony, that God gave us eternal life, and this life is in his Son. Whoever has the Son has life; whoever does not have the Son of God does not have life. *(1 John 5:11–12)*

That's quite a statement. Either you have Jesus (and life), or you don't. What about you? Do you have the Son? Do you have life? If you don't, what are you waiting for? There is no better time than right now to put your trust in Christ.

Study 4

John 3

We skip now all the way to the New Testament. Hundreds of years have passed, and now God's promised Messiah, Jesus, is on earth, having been born in Bethlehem. He is the most written about personage in history. And of all the things said about Him, the most well-known is a verse in our latest chapter.

For years many major sporting events featured a man in the crowd wearing a rainbow wig and holding up a simple sign. The wig was to draw the attention of viewers. It was pretty effective—multicolored hair was hard to miss at a staid golf tournament. The man's hope was that people would see the sign—with only "John 3:16" written on it—and that their curiosity would cause them to look up the Bible reference.

The rainbow wig man (his real name was Rollen Stewart) is not the only one who has seen that verse as "the Bible in miniature." Countless preachers and regular old Christians over the centuries have used it as a summary of not only the gospel but also of the entire biblical message.

And no wonder! Just look at it:

> "For God so loved the world, that he gave his only Son, that whoever believes in him should not perish but have eternal life."

It includes a little bit of everything—God, love, Jesus, belief, sin, hope, eternity. They're all there.

But in this study we want to look at not just verse 16, but the verses that surround it. As powerful as the verse is by itself, it is even more powerful when considered along with its context.

So let's begin where we normally do, at the start of the chapter.

> Now there was a man of the Pharisees named Nicodemus, a ruler of the Jews. This man came to Jesus by night and said to him, "Rabbi, we know that you are a teacher come from God, for no one can do these signs that you do unless God is with him."
>
> *(John 3:1–2)*

There's been a lot of speculation on these two verses, specifically, why was Nicodemus coming to Jesus at night? No one actually knows the answer, but it's interesting to ponder. Two leading theories are that Nicodemus did not want to be seen going to Jesus so he went at night, or that he wanted to have a longer conversation with the Savior and he knew that would be difficult during the daytime. Thematically, scholars point out that John often speaks in terms of light and darkness, and Nicodemus's nighttime visit represents his own state of spiritual darkness.

It is worth noting that Nicodemus—let's call him Nick for short—was a Pharisee. In almost every instance in the Bible, the Pharisees are the bad guys, but, at least in this story, we have a sympathetic Pharisee.

So who were the Pharisees? They were a group of legalistic Jews who strictly followed not just the laws of Moses, but also laws that they had made up over the years. To put it in more common terms, they were "holier than thou," and often hypocrites.

Nick prefaces his question with a compliment to Jesus, calling him a rabbi, which was significant, especially since Jesus was not formally trained as a rabbi, and admits that God must be on Jesus' side since Jesus has been going around doing all sorts of miracles. In response Jesus says something rather provocative.

> Jesus answered him, "Truly, truly, I say to you, unless one is born again he cannot see the kingdom of God." *(John 3:3)*

(Side note: Most everyone reading this will be way too young to remember the 1976 presidential campaign, but Jimmy Carter, who went on to win the election, caused quite a stir by calling attention to the fact that he was a "born again" Christian. A few years after the election someone said to me, "Remember a few years ago when Jimmy Carter invented the term 'born again'?" I had to laugh and tell my friend that the president had not invented the term—Jesus Himself did!)

Jesus' answer confused Nick, who asked, "How can a man be born when he is old? Can he enter a second time into his mother's womb and be born?" Apparently Pharisees were not much for poetic license and so Nicodemus had taken what Jesus said literally.

> Jesus answered, "Truly, truly, I say to you, unless one is born of water and the Spirit, he cannot enter the

kingdom of God. That which is born of the flesh is flesh, and that which is born of the Spirit is spirit. Do not marvel that I said to you, 'You must be born again.'" *(John 3:5–7)*

Just like the first part of this chapter, these verses have been debated over the years. Just what, exactly, does it mean to be born of "water and the Spirit"? I think this much is clear: The combination of water and the Spirit means purification. For instance, in Titus 3:5 we read, "[Jesus] saved us, not because of works done by us in righteousness, but according to his own mercy, by the *washing* and regeneration of the *Holy Spirit* …" (emphasis mine).

In Ezekiel 36 God says,

"I will sprinkle clean water on you, and you shall be clean from all your uncleanness … And I will give you a new heart, and a new spirit I will put within you. And I will remove the heart of stone from your flesh and give you a heart of flesh. And I will put my Spirit within you, and cause you to walk in my statutes and be careful to obey my rules." *(Ezekiel 36:25–27)*.

This combination of water and Spirit is a powerful one, able to cleanse us of all of our unrighteousness and empower us to live the kind of life that God wants us to and that we would want to.

The analogy of being born all over again is perfect: When we trust in Christ, we are made new creatures (see 2 Corinthians 5:17). Our lives begin again from scratch. We are given a new start. What a wonderful gift!

Let's pick up Jesus' answer at verse 14:

> And as Moses lifted up the serpent in the wilderness, so must the Son of Man be lifted up, that whoever believes in him may have eternal life.
>
> *(John 3:14–15)*

That no doubt begins to sound familiar, as verse 15—"that whoever believes in him may have eternal life"—is virtually repeated in the next, more famous, verse. But the first part of that, about Moses lifting up a serpent, might be unfamiliar to you. It would not, however, have been unfamiliar to its original hearer, Nicodemus. As a Jew, Nick would have known well the story to which Jesus is referring. In order to understand what Jesus has just said (and is about to say), we need to go back to the Old Testament.

You remember in our last study we read about the exodus of the Jews from Egypt. We pick up the story years later as Moses is leading his people through the wilderness. They have been traveling a long time and are beginning to be mad at God for their wanderings. We'll pick up the story in Numbers 21:

> From Mount Hor they set out by the way to the Red Sea, to go around the land of Edom. And the people became impatient on the way. And the people spoke against God and against Moses, "Why have you brought us up out of Egypt to die in the wilderness? For there is no food and no water, and we loathe this worthless food." Then the LORD sent fiery serpents among the people, and they bit the people, so that many people of Israel died. *(Numbers 21:4–6)*

During their travels, the Lord had graciously provided food for the Israelites—manna every morning (see Exodus 16). It sounds like a pretty good deal but rather than be grateful for God's provision, they instead grew tired of it and began to grumble (and aren't we often guilty of the same thing?). As a result, God sent poisonous snakes into their midst and some died. At that point, the Israelites' tune began to change.

> And the people came to Moses and said, "We have sinned, for we have spoken against the LORD and against you. Pray to the LORD, that he take away the serpents from us." *(Numbers 21:7a)*

I see their attitude as one of repentance. They realized they were wrong. They realized they had no business ordering God around, and they were sincerely sorry. I believe Moses saw it that way, too. What God does next is fascinating and gives us the context that both Nick and Jesus understood when Jesus uttered His most famous saying.

> So Moses prayed for the people. And the LORD said to Moses, "Make a fiery serpent and set it on a pole, and everyone who is bitten, when he sees it, shall live." So Moses made a bronze serpent and set it on a pole. And if a serpent bit anyone, he would look at the bronze serpent and live. *(Numbers 21:7b–9)*

What an interesting and unusual solution to the Israelites' situation. Their problem was with snakes, so how does God heal them? With a snake! (Only in this case, it was a bronze snake.) For the Israelites' part, they had only to look upon the bronze snake, lifted high upon a pole, and believe that God would heal them—and He did!

(By the way, can you think of when you have ever seen an image of a snake on a pole? The next time you see an ambulance you will notice one. Historians aren't sure how a serpent-entwined rod became associated with medicine and healing, but I'm pretty sure I know—it's this story!)

It is with that unusual backstory that Jesus compares Himself to a snake. Look again at John 3:14–15: "And as Moses lifted up the serpent in the wilderness, so must the Son of Man be lifted up, that whoever believes in him may have eternal life."

The comparison is no accident or coincidence. Jesus Himself is making the point that the bronze serpent was merely a picture of what He would do for all of mankind hundreds of years later. You remember that the same thing that was killing the Israelites—snakes—was used by God to heal them. That reminds me of what 2 Corinthians 5:21 says about Jesus: "For our sake he made him to be sin who knew no sin, so that in him we might become the righteousness of God." Our sin was killing us, but God allowed Christ, who was Himself sinless, to take on all of our guilt and become sin in order to save us.

What was required of the Israelites is now required of us: Understand that we have been "bitten" by sin and that we are going to die, unless we recognize our wrongdoing, repent, and look in faith upon God's provision—the Son, lifted up on the cross on our behalf.

It's with that background that we get to the crescendo:

> "For God so loved the world, that he gave his only Son, that whoever believes in him should not perish but have eternal life."

Have you ever wondered what the phrase "God so loved" means in this verse? As it turns out, the double meaning in the English matches the double meaning in the Greek (the language the Gospel of John was written in). "God so loved" can mean both a degree—"God loved us so much!"—or it can mean the way God loves us—"this is how God loved us." To put it another way, God's love for us was *so* big that He *gave* His only Son for us.

Verse 17 often gets overlooked due to its more famous preceding verse, but it tells us a wonderful truth about God. "For God did not send his Son into the world to condemn the world, but in order that the world might be saved through him."

Likewise, verse 18 tells us an important truth about ourselves, and something I think we often overlook. "Whoever believes in him is not condemned, but whoever does not believe is condemned already, because he has not believed in the name of the only Son of God." Here's how the ESV Study Bible expounds this verse:

> Those who do not believe and trust in Christ have neither a positive nor a neutral standing before God. They stand condemned already before God for their sins because they have not trusted God's solution for guilt, the only Son of God. This verse also refutes the assertion that a sincere person following any religion can have eternal life with God.

Belief is the solution for our problem, so to *not* believe puts us in certain jeopardy.

There is much more in the remainder of the chapter and you will profit from reading it. For our purposes, however, I just want to look at a few more verses near the end of the chapter.

In verse 23, John the Baptist is brought back into the story. You remember that he said of Christ, "Behold, the Lamb of God, who takes away the sin of the world!" (John 1:29). Here in this chapter he gives what I think is one of the best summations of how we need to live our lives. It's almost short enough to be a bumper sticker. Talking about Jesus, he said, "He must increase, but I must decrease." John the Baptist was talking about his own role as a prophet diminishing now that the One he was predicting had arrived. But I think it's also a good prescription for life once you have believed in Jesus: He must increase, and you must decrease. Christ needs to become more and more important in your life and your own selfish interests and desires need to take a back seat. He needs to truly be allowed to be the Lord of your life.

Lastly, we'll end (appropriately) on the final verse. It sums up the whole chapter.

> Whoever believes in the Son has eternal life, whoever does not obey the Son shall not see life, but the wrath of God remains on him. *(John 3:36)*

These words are awful and frightening—God's wrath is a horrible thing—but these words are also fantastic and hopeful—believing in Christ saves us. We are made new, born again, and given life eternal. How Christ accomplished this is the subject of our next chapter.

Study 5

Mark 15

Years ago there was a young man in my Young Life club named Jay. Jay went with us on a ski trip during the winter of his sophomore year where he heard the gospel story for the first time. Months later, he joined us at Young Life summer camp. One night during that week we heard the story of the cross. Afterwards, Jay wanted to speak to me. He was visibly excited.

"I get it!" he told me.

"Get what?" I asked.

"Now I finally understand how God dealt with our sin problem. I've been losing sleep about it since the ski trip. Now I get it—Christ died for me and for my sins so that I don't have to!"

During the ski trip six months earlier, Jay had clearly heard about his sin and his need for a Savior, but he had not grasped the entire story; there were still some loose ends in his mind. As a result, he was very concerned about his sin and worried about what, if anything, he could do to help himself.

In English class you may have learned the word *denouement*. It's a fancy word for the final part of a play or novel where the plot is resolved. The word is from the French, meaning to untie, and part of the word has its roots in the Latin for knot. So, you could say that the denouement is where the knots of a story are untied and everything finally makes sense; there is resolution.

In this chapter, we're going to see the denouement, not just of our six-session study, but of the entire biblical story. By the end of this study I hope that, like Jay, you're able to say, "I get it!" As the great Christmas hymn "O Little Town of Bethlehem" says about Christ's coming, "The hopes and fears of all the years / Are met in thee tonight."

We've been alluding to the events discussed in this chapter during the entire study. It is the story of Christ's death on the cross and His subsequent resurrection. While we will be looking at Mark's account, the story is told in each of the four Gospels—one of the only events that is covered in each of them (not even the Nativity can make that claim).

There are several key players in the story of the cross. The first of these is Pilate. He was the Roman governor of Israel. What in the world does that mean?

Well, Israel was a conquered nation. They had been taken over by the Romans. As a result, the political and military power of the country was in Roman hands and Pilate was the one in charge, representing Caesar. Pilate was not a Jew. In fact, if he worshipped anyone at all, it would be his boss, Caesar.

The next group of players in this story are the chief priests, elders, and the Council. While Israel was not a free country, they still had their own religious leaders and that's who these folks were.

Look at the first five verses of Mark 15:

> And as soon as it was morning, the chief priests held a consultation with the elders and scribes and the whole council. And they bound Jesus and led him away and delivered him over to Pilate. And Pilate asked him, "Are you the King of the Jews?" And he answered him, "You have said so." And the chief priests accused him of many things. And Pilate again asked him, "Have you no answer to make? See how many charges they bring against you." But Jesus made no further answer, so that Pilate was amazed.
> *(Mark 15:1–5)*

The charge that the religious leaders brought against Jesus was that He claimed to be the King of the Jews.

You will notice that Jesus did not deny it; instead, He only said, "You have said so." That's because Jesus was indeed the King of the Jews—and of everyone else!

But the Jewish leaders did not believe that and hoped that such a claim would get Jesus into legal trouble. You see, in the Roman Empire only Caesar was recognized as king. Everyone, regardless of religion, was to swear their allegiance to him.

The fact that Jesus did not defend Himself—only saying, "You have said so"—came as a real shock to Pilate. Roman law dictated that if an accused person did not defend himself, the judge—in this case, Pilate—had to find the person guilty!

There was something else going on that Pilate did not know was at play. Jesus was busy fulfilling Scripture. Hundreds of years earlier, God had given prophecies about the coming Messiah. One of them was met specifically in Jesus' action. Isaiah 53:7 says,

> He was oppressed, and he was afflicted,
>   yet he opened not his mouth;
> like a lamb that is led to the slaughter,
>   and like a sheep that before its shearers is silent,
>   so he opened not his mouth.

Of course this ties in exactly with our previous study where we learned that Jesus was the lamb of God. None of this was by accident!

We've met several players but the next one is arguably even more important: it's you! Actually, it's a guy named Barabbas, but he represents all of us, for reasons that will become clear as you read on.

We don't know a lot about Barabbas but what we do know does not paint a pretty picture: He was a murderer and an insurrectionist. He was in jail for good reason: He was guilty! In that sense, he is like we are: guilty before God of our sin and deserving of punishment.

That's not the only place where we bear a similarity with Barabbas.

> Now at the feast he used to release for them one prisoner for whom they asked. And among the rebels in prison, who had committed murder in the insurrection, there was a man called Barabbas. And the crowd came up and began to ask Pilate to do as he usually did for them. And he answered them, saying, "Do you want me to release for you the King of the Jews?" For he perceived that it was out of envy that the chief priests had delivered him up. *(Mark 15:6–10)*

Apparently Pilate had a tradition of releasing a prisoner of the people's choosing to the Jews during their celebration of Passover. Pilate was a quintessential politician: He wanted to please the crowd. So, he took the easy route. While he believed Jesus to be innocent, he did not have the courage to let him go free; instead he appealed to the crowd. I think he thought the crowd would demand to free Jesus. To hasten that decision, Pilate offered up as the only alternative someone who was the polar opposite of Jesus: Barabbas.

Whatever Pilate's motivations, the crowd was manipulated to ask for Barabbas. The religious leaders were jealous of the Savior and organized their community accordingly, creating a mob.

> But the chief priests stirred up the crowd to have him release for them Barabbas instead. And Pilate again said to them, "Then what shall I do with the man you call the King of the Jews?" And they cried out again, "Crucify him." And Pilate said to them, "Why, what evil has he done?" But they shouted all the more, "Crucify him." So Pilate, wishing to satisfy the crowd, released for them Barabbas, and having scourged Jesus, he delivered him to be crucified.
>
> *(Mark 15:11–15)*

No one (besides Christ) looks good in these verses. Pilate condemns an innocent man to death. The religious leaders are the ones who brought Jesus to trial in the first place and additionally they manipulated the crowd to get their way. Lastly, the people are guilty of crying out for Jesus—an innocent man—to be crucified.

Meanwhile, Barabbas, who was guilty in everyone's eyes, got off scot-free. Imagine what it was like for Barabbas to be yanked out of his jail cell and set free. He must have asked, "Why are you doing this?" And the response would have come back, "Jesus is dying in your place today." That is the ultimate way Barabbas is like us: He became the first person to understand what it meant to have Jesus die in his place.

Scourging was an awful procedure, also known as flogging, where prisoners were beat to within an inch of their lives. In fact, some prisoners of the time died from it.

> And the soldiers led him away inside the palace (that is, the governor's headquarters), and they called together the whole battalion. And they clothed him in a purple cloak, and twisting together a crown of thorns, they put it on him. And they began to salute

him, "Hail, King of the Jews!" And they were striking his head with a reed and spitting on him and kneeling down in homage to him. And when they had mocked him, they stripped him of the purple cloak and put his own clothes on him. And they led him out to crucify him. *(Mark 15:16–20)*

As if the physical torment was not enough, the soldiers then began to ridicule Jesus. Think about that for a moment: the very Son of God, the Creator of the Universe, was being mocked by His own creation. But Jesus had a mission to accomplish and nothing was going to deter Him from completing it. Since Jesus' supposed crime was claiming to be a king, the soldiers thought it would be fun to dress Him in purple, the traditional color of royalty, and to give Him a fake crown.

But of course, the worst was still to come. Crucifixion, the Roman government's favorite form of capital punishment, was horribly painful. The convicted criminal would be nailed by his hands and feet to a wooden cross (just think about what that must have been like!). They would then be left to die. The death would take hours, during which the criminal would be in excruciating pain—the word *excruciating* actually comes from the Latin word to crucify. (A side note: Sometimes

Christians go out of their way to make the claim that crucifixion is the most painful way that man has ever devised to kill another person. I don't know whether that's true or not. Man has shown no lack of creativity for inflicting pain on others down through the centuries. The important point of the pain of Christ's crucifixion is not that it set some sort of gruesome record; it's that He went through it, and did so for each of us.)

However painful the crucifixion was, Jesus did not want to avoid the pain.

> And they offered him wine mixed with myrrh, but he did not take it. *(Mark 15:23)*

Wine and myrrh would have acted as a primitive anesthetic to deaden the pain. Jesus did not want to forego the pain—He was experiencing in full the punishment that our sin deserved.

> So also the chief priests with the scribes mocked him to one another, saying, "He saved others; he cannot save himself. Let the Christ, the King of Israel, come down now from the cross that we may see and believe." Those who were crucified with him also reviled him. *(Mark 15:31–32)*

Here we have a return visit from the chief priests. They add to the mocking that the soldiers have already given Jesus. We also have the introduction in these verses of the next two characters in the story of that most important day: the thieves who were crucified alongside Jesus.

At first, both of the thieves were insulting Jesus, but one apparently had a change of heart. The details of his story are found in Luke:

> One of the criminals who were hanged railed at him, saying, "Are you not the Christ? Save yourself and us!" But the other rebuked him, saying, "Do you not fear God, since you are under the same sentence of condemnation? And we indeed justly, for we are receiving the due reward of our deeds; but this man has done nothing wrong." *(Luke 23:39–41)*

A beautiful thing happens in the next two verses: Jesus forgives the repentant thief:

> And he said, "Jesus, remember me when you come into your kingdom." And he said to him, "Truly, I say to you, today you will be with me in Paradise."
>
> *(Luke 23:42–43)*

The repentant thief's story is short yet there is so much in it for us to consider. You see that he recognized who Jesus was, that he repented from his previous, wrong attitude about Him, and that he came to Christ not as an equal, but as a sinner, acknowledging his need for mercy. He understood who Christ was, and he also understood who he was—a sinner, guilty and deserving of punishment. And Christ had mercy on him, personally guaranteeing the thief his place in heaven. The thief's response is exactly how we should respond as well.

Now we come to the most important hours in all of human history.

> And when the sixth hour had come, there was darkness over the whole land until the ninth hour. And at the ninth hour Jesus cried with a loud voice, "Eloi, Eloi, lema sabachthani?" which means, "My God, my God, why have you forsaken me?" *(Mark 15:33–34)*

Why did the world go dark for three hours when Jesus was on the cross? I believe it is because that is when Christ took upon Himself all of mankind's sin. God the Father turned His back on His Son. Here's how it is explained in Scripture:

> For God made Christ, who never sinned, to be the
> offering for our sin, so that we could be made right
> with God through Christ.   *(2 Corinthians 5:21, NLT)*

Other translations say that Christ actually became sin on our behalf. Think of that! The One who never sinned—"who knew no sin"—*became* sin itself on our behalf. He took *all* of our sin upon Himself. The reason Jesus was able to pay for our sins is because He had no sins of His own to pay for—"he knew no sin." None of us could have done that, no matter how good our intentions were, for we have our own sins to pay for.

To validate what Jesus had done, something amazing happened:

> And Jesus uttered a loud cry and breathed his last.
> And the curtain of the temple was torn in two, from
> top to bottom.   *(Mark 15:37–38)*

The curtain that was in the temple was a physical representation of man's separation from God. However, thanks to the sacrifice of Christ, we now have access to God directly. The sacrificial system we have talked about in earlier chapters was done away with: Christ died, once for all sins (see 1 Peter 3:18). It is no accident that 3:00 p.m. (approximately nine hours after sunrise, hence "the ninth hour" in biblical terms), the time that Jesus gave His final utterance from the cross, was the time that the afternoon sacrifices were made in the temple.

The story does not end there, even though the chapter does. The next six verses are needed to complete our story. Let's take a look at the first three of them:

> When the Sabbath was past, Mary Magdalene, Mary the mother of James, and Salome bought spices, so that they might go and anoint him. And very early on the first day of the week, when the sun had risen, they went to the tomb. And they were saying to one another, "Who will roll away the stone for us from the entrance of the tomb?" *(Mark 16:1–3)*

When you know how a story ends it's sometimes hard to appreciate what it felt like as it unfolded in real time. While we know what happened, no one then could have guessed the events to come. It's helpful to put yourself in their shoes. The women who went to the tomb were beside themselves with grief. It wasn't just that their friend had died. He had been violently arrested in the middle of the night, taken away from them, put through unfair trials, flogged, and finally murdered.

Now that the violence was over and the other side had won their victory, the least the women could do—really the only thing they could do—was to take care of the body and prepare Jesus for a proper burial. That's the task they set forth to do that morning.

In their haste and grief, perhaps, they had not stopped to consider a practical question: Who will roll away the stone? As they were pondering and worrying over this practicality, they became witnesses to the greatest miracle of all time.

> And looking up, they saw that the stone had been rolled back—it was very large. And entering the tomb, they saw a young man sitting on the right side, dressed in a white robe, and they were alarmed. And he said to them, "Do not be alarmed. You seek Jesus of Nazareth, who was crucified. He has risen; he is not here. See the place where they laid him."
>
> *(Mark 16:4–6)*

The women were startled at first. Understandable, isn't it? If you came to a tomb only to find it open, your friend's body nowhere to be found, and a stranger sitting inside, you would be scared, too! But the stranger (actually strangers, see Luke 24:4 and John 20:12) immediately took steps to calm them. Then these women became the first to hear the glorious words, "He has risen!"

They were looking for Jesus somewhere that He wasn't: among the dead. Jesus was no longer dead; He had risen. He was—and remains to this day—alive!

And this is the cornerstone of the Christian faith. Jesus not only paid for our sin, but He conquered death. He rose from the dead. Because He did, that means we can have eternal life as well (if Jesus had been defeated by death, then there could be no guarantee that we could live eternally). It means that we can have a relationship with Jesus today because He is still alive. It is also proof that God accepted Jesus' payment for our sin. The fact that He is risen is the game-changer of all time! If you don't understand that, you need to slow down a bit and think about it some more.

The Bible goes on to talk about many appearances by Jesus after His resurrection. There is ample proof that we worship a resurrected, *living* Savior.

Let's finish this study by going back to discussing the crucifixion. The cross and what took place there is the method by which we are made right with God. The cross is where God's love and His justice meet. Think about that. God is love (1 John 4:8). We all like that sentiment. But the Bible makes abundantly clear that He is also just. That means He must punish all wrongdoing. How can a *loving* God be perfectly *just*? It would seem that the two things cannot coexist.

Perhaps that's the problem that my young friend Jay, whom I mentioned at the start of this chapter, had. We want God to be loving. But we also need (and want) Him to be just. The cross and Jesus' selfless sacrifice there is the perfect (and really only) solution. It is the ultimate denouement. Here is how Jesus' friend Peter, who was an eyewitness on that fateful day, put it:

> [Jesus] personally carried our sins in his body on the cross so that we can be dead to sin and live for what is right. By his wounds you are healed. Once you were like sheep who wandered away. But now you have turned to your Shepherd, the Guardian of your souls. *(1 Peter 2:24–25, NLT)*

In our final chapter, we'll take a look at how the truth of Jesus' death and resurrection should impact the way we live and treat one another.

Study 6

Romans 12

Think back on all the Christmas and birthday gifts you have ever been given. What is the most valuable thing someone has ever given you? When they gave it to you, how did you show your appreciation?

I imagine the first thing you did was to say thanks. Then after that, at least for a while, you tried to make sure they knew that you appreciated the gift. Maybe you were even on your best behavior for a time.

You almost certainly did not shun the giver and pay no attention to them. No, typically, when we are truly grateful for someone's generosity, we show our appreciation by being a better friend, child, or "significant other" to the giver.

Can you see where I am going with this? Ultimately the greatest gift that we have ever been given, or ever can be given, is our new life in Christ thanks to His death for us on the cross. The Bible clearly tells us that

He did this because He loved us, and because we had no other chance for salvation.

So how do we go about showing our appreciation for what Christ has done for us? In this study we're going to take a look at one of my favorite chapters of Scripture: Romans 12. It is a great guide to how we can show our gratitude to the Lord for what He has done and is full of both spiritual and practical truths.

The first verse is a doozy that sets up the entire chapter.

> Therefore, I urge you, brothers, in view of God's mercy, to offer your bodies as living sacrifices, holy and pleasing to God—this is your spiritual act of worship. *(Romans 12:1, NIV 1984)*

There's a whole lot in that one verse, so we will need to pick it apart carefully. It speaks of God's mercy. Have you ever considered what mercy means? A common and correct definition is that mercy is *not* getting what we deserve. If you beg for a judge to have mercy on you, you are admitting your guilt but asking for him to be kind to you and not treat you as harshly as you deserve.

God has shown us His mercy by forgiving us through Christ. We do not get the punishment we deserve because God recognizes Christ's payment in our stead.

The first verse in Romans 12 is saying, "Now that you understand God's mercy, you need to offer your very selves as a spiritual sacrifice."

In this book we have talked a lot about sacrificial offerings. They're one of the main themes of the Bible. We have talked about the ultimate sacrifice—that of Jesus on the cross for us—but we have also talked about the sacrifice all the way back in Genesis of the animals for Adam and Eve's clothes, and also the Passover sacrifice.

Can you see the one thing those three sacrifices—Jesus, the animals, and the scapegoat—all had in common? They all had to die!

In all that follows in this chapter, we are to remember that Christ died for us, that He gave His life for us, and therefore we need to live accordingly.

Verse 1 calls us to be "living sacrifices." Unlike those other sacrifices we're not to physically die but to actively live out our lives for the Lord. Then it says that our lives are to be "holy and pleasing to God." How in the world do we do that? The next verse gives us some insight:

> Do not conform any longer to the pattern of this world, but be transformed by the renewing of your mind. Then you will be able to test and approve what God's will is—his good, pleasing and perfect will.
>
> *(Romans 12:2, NIV 1984)*

So one of the first things we need to do is to reorder our thinking. No longer should we let the world and its values (or lack thereof) dictate to us how we should live and what we should hold important. Just look at the world around you. Listen for a moment to the evening news or the latest hit movie or TV show with this question in mind: Does the world around you follow Jesus? No way! Quite the opposite. No, we are to let the Lord renew—literally "make new"—our minds.

Have you ever stopped to consider the connection between our mind and our actions? Our actions get their start in our minds, right? If we can control our minds, then we can control our actions. This verse is telling us to let God make our minds new so that we will behave the way He wants us to, rather than the way the world wants us to.

The way that we renew our minds is by listening more to what God says than to what the world says. The single most important thing in this regard is to spend time in God's Word. How is that important? I'll illustrate it with a story.

I've had lots of friends who have moved from other parts of the country and the world to Texas where I live. After a while, they go back home to visit. Invariably, their old friends and family say, "What's happened? You sound like you're from Texas!" That's because, without even knowing it, their time in the Lone Star State has influenced the way they speak.

That's the way we need to be with God's Word. We need to be in it enough that someone will notice that we begin to speak with a new accent—in this case not a Texas accent but a Jesus accent! That new "accent" needs to permeate every area of our lives.

Of course there are other things that can help us "change our accent": spending time with other Christians in fellowship, being involved in Christian service and activity, and also spending time in prayer. All of those things will "renew our minds." As our minds will be made new, then our outward behavior will change. And often, like my non-Texan friends, we may even change without noticing that we're changing!

Keep in mind that the reverse is true, too. The longer you stay away from God's Word and His things, the more your old "accent" will come back. We need to constantly be being renewed. Second Corinthians 4:16 says, "Our inner self is being renewed day by day," and that is how we should be. Renewing our minds is all about putting God's thoughts into our heads, rather than the world's thoughts.

Why would we want to do that? Other than the fact that it's what God commands of us, there's also a really cool truth that verse 2 points out. God's will is "good, pleasing, and perfect."

I don't know about you, but if I could be guaranteed to make decisions that were good, pleasing, and perfect, I'd sign up in a heartbeat! Well, that's exactly what we get when we do God's will. His will is always good, pleasing, and perfect. It may not be easy or convenient, but it's always right.

Following verse 2, Paul, the author of Romans, goes on to give us some instructions on how we can live a life that pleases God.

> For by the grace given me I say to every one of you: Do not think of yourself more highly than you ought, but rather think of yourself with sober judgment, in accordance with the measure of faith God has given you. *(Romans 12:3, NIV 1984)*

One of the reasons I like Romans 12 so much is that it is full of practical instruction and this verse is an example. We should have a *realistic* understanding of who we are—neither too high nor too low. We should see ourselves as God sees us. We are indeed wonderfully made (Psalm 139:14) but we are also sinners, every one of us (Romans 3:23). Don't insult God by ignoring your own faults, nor insult Him by denigrating what He has made in His image!

We should also work together with other Christians, as the next verses discuss.

> Just as each of us has one body with many members, and these members do not all have the same function, so in Christ we who are many form one body, and each member belongs to all the others. We have different gifts, according to the grace given us. If a man's gift is prophesying, let him use it in proportion to his faith. If it is serving, let him serve; if it is teaching, let him teach; if it is encouraging, let him encourage; if it is contributing to the needs of others, let him give generously; if it is leadership, let him govern diligently; if it is showing mercy, let him do it cheerfully. *(Romans 12:4–8, NIV 1984)*

In this great passage, Paul uses the analogy of a human body, where there are many parts that make up the one body. He lists several gifts in those four verses, known as "spiritual gifts." The Bible tells us that God has gifted each believer to do something for His Body, the church. Learning what your spiritual gift is, and then putting it to practice, will be a big help to you in your Christian experience.

(The gifts are talked about here in Romans and also in 1 Corinthians 12:7–10; 1 Corinthians 12:28; and Ephesians 4:11. A full study of the gifts is beyond the scope of this little book but highly encouraged.)

Christianity is such a positive religion! God gives us gifts. We are to work together, in harmony, building up the Body of Christ. We all have value to the larger group, and they to us. All of us can serve the Lord.

Now he goes on to talk about other ways that we need to live out our faith. Here's a short one:

> Love must be sincere. Hate what is evil; cling to what is good. *(Romans 12:9, NIV 1984)*

The Bible talks an awful lot about love so it might be good to know just what love is. It's interesting to ask people to define it; they almost always have a hard time doing so. Here's a wonderful definition that I learned a long time ago that I think sums it up well: *Love is always wanting what's best for the other person.* But just knowing the definition doesn't make loving others any easier. Love is hard work!

In that one little verse Paul gives us two commands: 1) our love must be sincere; and 2) we are to hate what is evil while holding on to what is good. The way to determine if something is evil or not is to judge it by God's standards, not man's. As we get to know Christ more, He will make clear to us what His standards are, largely through His Word.

If I was set adrift in the middle of the ocean and all I had was a life raft, I can guarantee you that I would not stray away from that raft! I wouldn't go off for a leisurely swim in the afternoon, hoping the raft would still be there when I returned. No, I would cling to it as if my life depended on it. Why? Because my life *would* depend on it (they don't call them life rafts for nothing!)

We are to hate what is evil and cling to what is good. Clinging onto the good things—things that will draw us to Christ, not keep us away from Him—will keep us alive, spiritually. They are our spiritual life rafts. One of those things we should cling on to is fellowship with other believers. Paul addresses that in verse 10:

> Be devoted to one another in brotherly love. Honor one another above yourselves.
>
> *(Romans 12:10, NIV 1984)*

That's a hard one to do, because it requires us to be unselfish. But wouldn't the world be better if all of us believers would live it out?

> Never be lacking in zeal, but keep your spiritual fervor, serving the Lord. Be joyful in hope, patient in affliction, faithful in prayer.
>
> *(Romans 12:11–12, NIV 1984)*

Remember these verses when walking with Christ becomes difficult, as it no doubt will. Jesus did not promise an easy life, far from it. These verses are a good prescription for how to hang in there when the going gets tough.

The next several verses continue the discussion of how we are to treat others:

> Share with God's people who are in need. Practice hospitality. Bless those who persecute you; bless and do not curse. Rejoice with those who rejoice; mourn with those who mourn. Live in harmony with one

another. Do not be proud, but be willing to associate with people of low position. Do not be conceited.
(Romans 12:13–16, NIV 1984)

There is much to think about in those verses. Some of those things are not easy to do! When we are faced with something God wants us to do that is difficult, we should ask Him for His help. God wants us to succeed and bring Him glory in these things. He does not expect us to do them on our own. Far from it. He wants to be involved in every aspect of our lives. Ask for His help in treating others as He would have us do.

The last verses in this chapter talk about how to deal specifically with people who treat you wrongly.

> Do not repay anyone evil for evil. Be careful to do what is right in the eyes of everybody. If it is possible, as far as it depends on you, live at peace with everyone. Do not take revenge, my friends, but leave room for God's wrath, for it is written: "It is mine to avenge; I will repay," says the Lord. On the contrary: "If your enemy is hungry, feed him; if he is thirsty, give him something to drink. In doing this, you will heap burning coals on his head." Do not be overcome by evil, but overcome evil with good. *(Rom. 12:17–21, NIV 1984)*

As if the Lord had not already given us enough to do in this chapter, He ends it with some of the most challenging directions yet!

The fact of the matter is that people can be jerks. The Bible does not ignore this fact and paint humanity as if it was wonderful. It is not. Not even Christians are perfect—we just know Someone who is. Until we're in heaven, we're going to treat others unkindly and have others treat us poorly. We are sinful human beings.

But revenge is best left to God. Remember, Christ even told us to "turn the other cheek" (see Luke 6:29).

Going back to the very start of this final study, we are to live our lives in view of what Christ has done for us (Romans 12:1). We cannot do enough for Him. He held nothing back for us and we should hold nothing back for Him. We should live our lives as living sacrifices, giving everything we have over to Him. It is only in so doing that you will live life the way it was meant to be lived.

The six chapters of Scripture we studied in this book are only a snippet of what the Bible has for you. There is so much more. Hebrews 4:12 tells us that "the word of God is living and active. Sharper than any double-edged sword, it penetrates even to dividing soul and spirit, joints and marrow; it judges the thoughts and attitudes of the heart" (NIV 1984). My hope for you is that you spend a lifetime studying it and letting its words guide you. If you do that, then—and only then—will you experience "life to the full" (John 10:10).

About the Author

Kit Sublett lives in Houston, Texas, where he served on the staff of Young Life for twenty years. He is the editor of numerous books as well as the author of several other books written to help people grow in their Christian faith. He considers *The Diaries of Jim Rayburn* (Young Life's founder) to be his *magnum opus*. He is a graduate of Trinity University. Follow him on Twitter @kitsublett. He can be reached through the publisher at ran@whitecapsmedia.com.

Colophon

Book designed by Randolph McMann for Whitecaps Media

Main body composed in Chaparral Pro Regular 10.5/15. Chaparral Pro was created by Adobe designer Carol Twombly

Cover designed by Stephanie W. Dicken

426 Series editor: Kit Sublett

Be sure to visit
whitecapsmedia.com
for more
426 Series Bible studies
and the Study Guide
for this book

www.ingramcontent.com/pod-product-compliance
Ingram Content Group UK Ltd.
Pitfield, Milton Keynes, MK11 3LW, UK
UKHW021322180426
11947UKWH00017B/1389